Level Three

PETER and the WOLF

by SERGE PROKOFIEV
arranged by WESLEY SCHAUM

for
PIANO

PETER AND THE WOLF, OP. 67 by Sergei Prokofiev
© Copyright 1937 (Renewed) by G. Schirmer, Inc. (ASCAP) for the U.S., Canada and Mexico
International Copyright Secured • All Rights Reserved • Used by Permission

EXCLUSIVELY DISTRIBUTED BY

HAL•LEONARD®
CORPORATION
7777 W. BLUEMOUND RD. P.O. BOX 13819 MILWAUKEE, WI 53213

**Serge Prokofiev
(1891-1953)**

Foreword

This delightful tale relates the triumph of Peter's adventuresome spirit and ingenuity over the evil wolf. In its original orchestral version, each of the principal characters were represented by a different musical instrument, thereby providing a chance for youngsters to become familiar with the sounds of these instruments.

The story and music were written in 1938 by Serge Prokofiev, now generally considered to have been one of the most outstanding composers in contemporary Russia.

As with many modern composers, Prokofiev used familiar and traditional harmonies spiced and flavored with dissonances that helped create stunning dramatic efforts. Many such examples will be found here. Thus, the pupil is given the opportunity to experience some contemporary sounds in music. The familiar adage, "Dissonance is like a tack - don't sit on it," is good advice to the student who may pick out isolated dissonances and wince. Of course, the music is intended to flow along, without pausing at dissonant intervals.

There is considerable potential for recital use. The narration of the story could be told by the pupil playing the piano or by a second student. If more than one piano is available, different pupils might play various parts of the music. Use costumes for added dramatic effect. Invite audience participation in the thematic quiz at the conclusion. The entire presentation has many possibilities for music appreciation groups and classrooms.

The pupil gains many sight-reading benefits while learning the pieces in this book. Much use is made of changing clefs and different types of accompaniment patterns.

Early one morning Peter opened the gate and went out into the big green meadow.

PETER'S THEME

Giocoso M.M. ♩ = 152–168

On the branch of a big tree sat a little bird, Peter's friend. "All is quiet," chirped the bird gaily.

BIRD'S THEME
Arioso M.M. ♩ = 160 – 176

Soon a duck came waddling around. She was glad that Peter had not closed the gate, and decided to take a nice swim in the deep pond in the meadow.

DUCK'S THEME

6

Seeing the duck, the little bird flew down upon the grass, settled next to the duck and shrugged his shoulders. "What kind of a bird are you, if you can't fly!" he said. To this the duck replied, "What kind of a bird are you, if you can't swim!" and dived into the pond. They argued and argued — the duck swimming in the pond, the little bird hopping along the shore.

BIRD AND DUCK ARGUE

Suddenly something caught Peter's attention. He noticed a cat crawling thru the grass.

CAT'S THEME

The cat thought: "The bird is busy arguing. I'll just grab her." Stealthily she crept toward the bird on her velvet paws.

CAT CREEPS UP ON BIRD

"Look out!" shouted Peter, and the bird immediately flew up in the tree, while the duck quacked angrily at the cat from the middle of the pond

CAT POUNCES BUT BIRD ESCAPES

The cat crawled around the tree and thought: "Is it worth climbing up so high? By the time I get there the bird will have flown away."

CAT THINKS IT OVER

* Play both notes with thumb

Grandfather came out. He was angry because Peter had gone into the meadow. "It is a dangerous place. If a wolf should come out of the forest, then what would you do?"

GRANDFATHER'S THEME

Maestoso M.M. ♩=108-126

Peter paid no attention to grandfather's words. Boys such as he are not afraid of wolves.

PETER IGNORES GRANDFATHER

But grandfather took Peter by the hand, led him home and locked the gate.

GRANDFATHER PREVAILS

No sooner had Peter gone, than a big grey wolf came out of the forest.

WOLF'S THEME
Misterioso M.M. ♩=80-92

In a twinkling, the cat climbed up the tree.

CAT CLIMBS INTO TREE
Allegretto M.M. ♩=84–96

The duck quacked, and in her excitement jumped out of the pond.

DUCK JUMPS OUT OF WATER
Vivace M.M. ♩=92–112

But no matter how hard the duck tried to run, she couldn't escape the wolf. He was getting nearer and nearer. Then he got her, and with one gulp swallowed her.

DUCK RUNS BUT IS CAUGHT BY WOLF

And now, this is how things stood: the cat was sitting on one branch, the bird on another — not too close to the cat.

CAT AND BIRD SHARE TREE BRANCH

Leggiero M.M. ♩=84-96

And the wolf walked around and around the tree, looking at them with greedy eyes.

WOLF LOOKS UP GREEDILY

Misterioso M.M. ♩=80-92

In the meantime, Peter, without the slightest fear, stood behind the closed gate watching all that was going on.

PETER WATCHES

He ran home, took a strong rope and climbed up the stone wall. One of the branches of the tree, around which the wolf was walking, stretched out over the wall. Grabbing hold of the branch, Peter lightly climbed over onto the tree.

PETER CLIMBS INTO TREE

Peter said to the bird, "Fly down and circle around the wolf's head; only take care that he doesn't catch you."

PETER TALKS TO BIRD

The bird almost touched the wolf's head with his wings, while the wolf snapped angrily at him from this side and that. How the bird did worry the wolf! How he wanted to catch him! But the bird was more clever, and the wolf simply couldn't do anything about it.

WOLF TRIES TO GET BIRD

Meanwhile, Peter made a lasso and, carefully letting it down, caught the wolf by the tail and pulled with all his might.

PETER LOWERS LASSO
Misterioso M.M. ♩=160–176

Feeling himself caught, the wolf began to jump wildly trying to get loose.

WOLF TRIES TO GET LOOSE
Agitato M.M. ♩=84–96

But Peter tied the other end of the rope to the tree, and the wolf's jumping only made the rope around his tail tighter.

WOLF IS CAUGHT

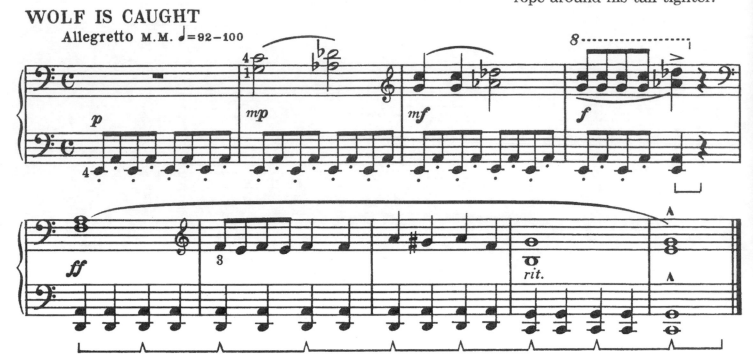

Just then, some hunters came out of the woods, following the wolf's trail and shooting as they went.

HUNTERS' THEME

(Hunters shoot guns)

But Peter, sitting in the tree, said: "Don't shoot! Birdie and I have already caught the wolf. Now help us take him to the zoo."

PETER CALLS TO HUNTERS

Imagine the triumphant procession. Peter at the head, and after him, the hunters leading the wolf. Above them flew the little bird, chirping boastfully about their catch.

PROCESSIONAL

And if one would listen very carefully, he could hear the duck quacking inside the wolf. Because in his hurry, the wolf had swallowed her alive.

DUCK'S REQUIEM

Peter and the Wolf – THEMATIC QUIZ

Directions: Below are seven different themes used in "Peter and the Wolf". Match each melody with the character it represents by placing the number of the theme on the line along side of the proper sketch.